I0102753

Strategic Studies Institute
and
U.S. Army War College Press

DEFENSE PLANNING FOR NATIONAL SECURITY: NAVIGATION AIDS FOR THE MYSTERY TOUR

Colin S. Gray

March 2014

The views expressed in this report are those of the author and do not necessarily reflect the official policy or position of the Department of the Army, the Department of Defense, the U.S. Government, Her Majesty's Government, the UK Ministry of Defence, or the Royal Navy. Authors of Strategic Studies Institute (SSI) and U.S. Army War College (USAWC) Press publications enjoy full academic freedom, provided they do not disclose classified information, jeopardize operations security, or misrepresent official U.S. policy. Such academic freedom empowers them to offer new and sometimes controversial perspectives in the interest of furthering debate on key issues.

*****

FOREWORD

Defense planning unavoidably must be in the nature of a mystery tour. The inability to know the future is a permanent condition for defense planning, but it is one with which we must cope. This monograph by Dr. Colin S. Gray explores and examines the implications of our irreducible ignorance about the future. His purpose is to identify an approach to this critically important subject of security that leans heavily upon what we can and should know about the past and present, in order to anticipate future conditions.

The monograph finds that, although the past does not repeat itself in detail, there are profound persisting reasons why it is repeated approximately in the challenges and dangers that security communities must face. Dr. Gray concludes that notwithstanding the facts of contextual change in strategic history, the "great stream of time" from the past, through the present, into the future commands critically significant continuities in history that yield an approach to the future in which some confidence can be placed.

DOUGLAS C. LOVELACE, JR.
Director
Strategic Studies Institute and
    U.S. Army War College Press

ABOUT THE AUTHOR

COLIN S. GRAY is Professor of International Politics and Strategic Studies at the University of Reading, England. He worked at the International Institute for Strategic Studies in London, UK and at the Hudson Institute in Croton-on-Hudson, NY before founding the National Institute for Public Policy, a defense-oriented think tank in the Washington, DC, area. Dr. Gray served for 5 years in the Ronald Reagan administration on the President's General Advisory Committee on Arms Control and Disarmament. A dual citizen of the United States and UK, he has served as an adviser to both the U.S. and British governments. His government work has included studies of nuclear strategy, arms control, maritime strategy, space strategy, and special forces. Dr. Gray has written 26 books, including: *The Sheriff: America's Defense of the New World Order* (University Press of Kentucky, 2004); *Another Bloody Century: Future Warfare* (Weidenfeld and Nicolson, 2005); *Strategy and History: Essays on Theory and Practice* (Routledge, 2006); *Fighting Talk: Forty Maxims on War, Peace and Strategy* (Potomac Books, 2009); *National Security Dilemmas: Challenges and Opportunities* (Potomac Books, 2009); *The Strategy Bridge: Theory for Practice* (Oxford University Press, 2010); *War, Peace and International Relations: An Introduction to Strategic History*, 2nd Ed. (Routledge, 2011); *Airpower for Strategic Effect* (Air University Press, 2012); and *Perspectives on Strategy* (Oxford University Press [OUP] 2013), which is the follow on to *Strategy Bridge*. The final volume in the *Strategy Bridge* trilogy, entitled *Strategy and Defence Planning*, will be published by OUP in 2014. Dr. Gray is a graduate of the Universities of Manchester and Oxford.

SUMMARY

The purpose of this monograph is to explore and examine the challenge to America's defense planners of needing to make purposeful and prudent choices in military preparation for the future. The problem for defense planning that is beyond resolution is the scientifically certain fact that we have no data from the future about the future. Moreover, this will always be a fact. No matter the scholarly discipline and tradition to which a defense planner owes or feels most allegiance, he or she needs to recognize and attempt to understand fully a personal and institutional condition of awesome ignorance of detail about the future.

Further study, more cunning analytical methodology, even more powerful computers—none of these can reveal with any certainty what the future will bring. Fortunately, this does not mean that we are ignorant about the future; but it does mean that defense planning is guesswork and can only be such. Understandably, both senior policymakers and soldiers tend to be reluctant, even to the point of appearing to be evasive, when legislators question the plausibility of the answers given in congressional hearings. After all, it can be troubling to the conscience of honest and competent people to be obliged to affirm the integrity of choices made in defense preparation for national security in years to come, when there is and can be no certain way to know that one is sufficiently correct.

DEFENSE PLANNING FOR NATIONAL SECURITY: NAVIGATION AIDS FOR THE MYSTERY TOUR

Purpose and Problems.

The purpose of this monograph is to explore and examine the challenge to America's defense planners of needing to make purposeful and prudent choices in military preparation for the future. The problem for defense planning that is beyond resolution is the scientifically certain fact that we have no data from the future about the future. Moreover, this will always be a fact. No matter the scholarly discipline and tradition to which a defense planner owes allegiance, he or she needs to recognize and attempt to understand fully a personal and institutional condition of awesome ignorance of detail about the future. Further study, more cunning analytical methodology, yet more powerful computers — none of these can reveal with any certainty what the future will bring. Fortunately, this does not mean that we are ignorant about the future; but it does mean that defense planning is guesswork and can only be such. Understandably, senior policymakers as well as soldiers tend to be reluctant, even to the point of appearing to be evasive, when legislators question the plausibility of the answers given in congressional hearings. After all, it can be troubling to the conscience of honest and competent people to be obliged to affirm the integrity of choices made in defense preparation for national security in years to come, when there is and can be no certain way to know that one is sufficiently correct.

My intention here is not to argue or even imply that there are ways in which the fog that shrouds the future can be lifted: It can't be and therefore I won't!

But, the future is knowable to us in important—albeit limited—respects, provided we adopt and accept the concept of there always being a great "stream of time."[1] The problem of ignorance about the future is one of physics among others, and has to be accepted as existential reality. It has to follow that, once honest acknowledgement of ignorance is made, the next step should be the positive one of enquiry as to what we do think that we know well enough for it to be pressed into contemporary service as analytical argument to aid prudent defense planning. One needs to accept as a working proposition the notably grand idea that there is a unity to time and our strategic history in it, with respect to which the defining quality of the future is only the inarguable fact that it has yet to happen. In other words, past, present, and future are a unitary phenomenon or quality. Acceptance of this idea has profound implications for a sensible approach to defense planning. The claim is not that history repeats itself, but it is that situations of concern to strategists endeavoring to conduct defense planning do recur and repeat generically over time.[2] Later sections of this monograph suggest what can be learned from history, as well as what cannot. However, it is essential to understand why the past and the present can be of assistance in planning defense preparation for the future.

Although the future is always a *tabula rasa* concerning the detail, including vital detail, of what will happen, the human security condition is anything but unknown, let alone unknowable. A key to making progress here is to pose only answerable questions. For a leading example of a foolish question, one should never ask "What will happen?" Reliable answers cannot be given with the certainty required of science.

When the subject encompasses war and warfare in its many variants, major and minor, the folly of bids to achieve a predictive quality to forecasts becomes readily apparent. Policy intended to promote domestic well-being can be difficult to design, develop, and sustain, but when compared and contrasted with the challenge inescapable from defense planning, it begins to appear almost modest. Defense planning must strive to cope not only with the major challenge posed by contingency—after all, that affects any and all areas—but also by the purposefully adversarial thought and behavior that must always attend the focus of this monograph.[3] The problem for defense planning is not only that posed by nature, which is to say a future that in a sense and by scientific definition can never arrive; in malign addition, it is the problem of the necessity to be ready enough to meet those who intend to thwart and harm us. Therefore, defense planning has to be seen and approached both as a challenge to guess prudently about things that cannot be known, and also as a challenge to guess prudently in conditions wherein we must expect to be opposed. Hard science, soft social science, and the humanities, are none of them, severally or together, capable of telling us what we really need to know about the future.[4] Unfortunately, perhaps, the duty of purposeful defense planning for future national security is not discretionary as an undertaking. It has to be done, at least attempted, by us, regardless of our ignorance.

I do not have the luxury of choosing a methodology from a shortlist of strongly attractive candidates. The past and the present are all that we have. The questions with practical meaning concern the utility of historical experience, bearing firmly in mind that that is the sole resource we can access. In its organization, this enquiry proceeds first with an explanation of the approach preferred, as well as a necessary explanation of why other potentially leading approaches have not been selected. Next, the monograph explains in some detail why strategy is the best suited and most adaptable methodology for the educational preparation of our contemporary defense planners. From theory, the monograph advances into the potentially contentious zone of "lessons" and caveats that may be derived carefully from experience in the past. I explain that this cannot be a scientific exercise, because we are able only to illustrate with historical examples what appear to be important general truths from experience, presented cautiously as lessons.[5] Finally, this monograph concludes with recommendations for serious consideration by the U.S. Army in its necessary commitment to plan prudently for the future.

Approaches.

Without apology, I will consider seriously only four approaches to defense planning. These leading four are considered inclusively and in a manner tolerant of some attempted borrowings from one category by another. My selected candidates are categorized as: (1) educated futurology; and (2) humanities (with particular reference to politics, history, and strategy). Because strategy is judged to provide the most useful approach to educational preparation for defense planning, at least when historical experience is accessed in a disciplined way, its substantial examination—as strategic history—is deferred for concentrated scrutiny until the next section. Following these largely methodological analyses of approaches to the hunt for useful theory, the monograph addresses the question directly, "What should the U.S. Army be able to learn that is worth learning from historical experience?" This weighty section offers suggested "lessons" that illustrate significantly how and why strategic history has moved in the past and moves in the present. This is not and cannot be scientific proof of what succeeds and what fails. But, it does yield important candidate "lessons," when considered broadly by category of event, episode, or situation. These lessons are not suggested as being of analogical merit in detail, but only of value for what the challenges in future strategic history could well pose and therefore need to be planned for.

1. **Educated futurology**. This very inclusive category of methods is intended to shine lamps upon what otherwise is a rather embarrassingly dark, in the sense of unknown, future. It may be worth noting that I choose to draw a distinction between educated and uneducated futurology. I must confess to some subjectivity in making this distinction. By "educated," I mean that the relevant defense planners have sought to employ methods that might contribute to their understanding of the future. Undeniably, the pertinent judgment is highly subjective. To be specific, I exclude divine revelation, astrology, and other prophesy from my shortlist of ways to be "educated" about the future. However, I do recognize that many people sincerely have faith in these methods. Even more to the point, I must admit that I cannot possibly prove with scientific certainty that anyone's vision of the future is either correct or not, regardless of their preferred method. In our pride as contemporary legatees of the spirit and much of the method of the Enlightenment, we tend to be so respectful of science and its values that we are willing to condone exaggeration of its possibili-

ties and suppress or ignore what we ought to know are its enduring limitations. One of the largest, if not the largest and most significant, of these weaknesses pertains to the future per se.

There is much disciplinary prejudice that fuels disdain for data and methods alien to those approved in their particular tribe of scholars. Also, there is simply the human fact that particular careers attract and require particular kinds of expertise. Few people are polymaths; even if they have the intellectual and cultural potential to be such, they simply do not have the time, relatively early in their careers. This means that some extremely demanding tasks are assigned to, and chosen probably unwisely by, people who are notably lacking in the knowledge and method to do well with them. It can be impossibly challenging for a highly pragmatic problem solving soldier to adjust mentally to meet the demands of defense planning. Perhaps the most difficult of cultural shifts required is the need to recognize, really recognize that the future is and must always be *terra incognita* in many respects. Understandably, the heroic demands made of official defense planners stimulate an urgent, not to say desperate, requirement for expertise in a method that may enable them to penetrate the future.

The sad realization that the future is impregnable to assault; that we do not have and cannot grow and nurture experts on the future, does not always reach the minds in need of this epiphany. As a result, hope springs eternal, notwithstanding the abundant evidence of failure. This author has heard senior people in several countries talk with wholly unmerited confidence about a "foreseeable future," when the condition that they envisaged inevitably was only the product of guesswork. Even that sometimes owed more to possibly inspirational insight, than to anything approximating scientific method.[6]

Accepting some risk of being unfair to substantively expert and methodologically competent scholars, it is important to signal the fragility, at best, of the defense analysis that underpins much of our future defense preparation. It may seem ungenerous to be critical of methods that have been designed and developed over many years, certainly since the Kennedy administration peopled the Office of the Secretary of Defense with graduates from the RAND Corporation.[7] However, this monograph must insist upon stating that the problems for American defense planners could not and cannot be solved by the methods of science, let alone social science. To cut to the chase: Defense planning must support requirements that will flow in matters both large and small from America's future strategic history. That history will be determined by political and strategic discretionary decisions, as well as by contingencies, that are intensely human and are both domestic and foreign. America's strategic future cannot be ours alone to determine and, need one say it, we expect it to be a narrative that does not have a concluding or conclusive grand objective. In other words, answer to the "When?" question about future strategic history, is literally beyond feasibility of answer. Not much of this is encouraging for aspiring futurologists in the U.S. Army or elsewhere.

a. Scenarios. Readers of this monograph probably will be familiar with, or have played some scenarios designed to illustrate future possibilities.[8] Such exercises can be well-conducted, and the imagination may be stretched productively. The first-order effects of possible contingencies may be enriched vitally, if not scarily, by identification of plausible second and even third order effects. This is an exercise that reminds participating players, as well as an audience of official "students," that strategy is really all about consequences. However, it can be the case that the sheer intensity of exposure to defense scenarios, on top of the sense of familiarity that scenarios encourage, combine to inspire a confidence in foreknowledge that is seriously, possibly fatally, misleading. After all, no matter how expertly designed and conducted, scenarios are only invented and therefore hypothetical futures, intended properly to serve only heuristic purposes. I have heard American defense officials express undeserved confidence in and about the relative safety and effectiveness of possible actions, on the basis of evidence admitted to be only scenario-based (e.g. "We have gamed this many times and it always/ usually worked!").

b. Trend spotting. If scenarios have the potential to seduce their inventors and players, one must also express a cautionary note about the almost irresistible, though typically unwarranted, respect accorded to future trend spotting.[9] Given that there is no data available from the future about the future, or even about the consequences of today, that could be regarded as certain or even useful, studies of future trends are, of necessity, gloriously liberated from fact. However, in the absence of data imagination can run riot. In practice, trend spotting efforts by official authors tend not to roam far from established fashion in beliefs. One would appear both irresponsible and professionally inexpert were one to prophecy a radical departure from the strategic context projected to be most likely and accepted today de facto as authoritative. The trouble for a defense planner is to decide whether or not what is an authoritative assumption today about tomorrow will be similarly in charge in the future. And then, of course, there is the disturbing thought that the "future" is a temporal concept utterly undisciplined by statute. How far into the future should one try to peer? How far can one see with any confidence? And, dare one ask, how far would be useful? In official practice, government finds itself all but inevitably obliged to be hugely conservative in its trend-spotting. Radical change is anathema to the orderly and usually incremental world of official business. There are three very substantial reasons why official trend projection inherently is prone to the error of undue conservatism.

(1) Responsible-looking analysis typically and understandably starts from a current condition. A trend therefore is anchored, if not weighted heavily, by where we are now.

(2) Although trends can be cumulatively radical in quality, the concept systemically flags continuity rather than discontinuity. Radical or not, trends are by definition linear rather than nonlinear in nature.

(3) The assumption of significant linearity in the concept of trend essentially is hostile to the notion of surprise, let alone the legitimacy of the concept of the "Black Swan" event that is all but entirely unexpected, yet which has profound lasting consequences on the course of strategic history.[10]

Trends are especially dangerous when projected out into the future, because in that case, familiar caution about uncertain or absent evidence needs to be especially strong, whereas more typically, it is weak. The very idea of a trend implies, indeed requires, the presence of several or many similar happenings. The fact that one is projecting the occurrence in a trend of categorically like phenomena can lend a plausibility that the prediction of a single event in isolation would lack. If one is sufficiently confident to identify and project a stream of similar things, people will be inclined to give them credit that may be undeserved. The temporal historical context in a trend is itself a source of evidence, even if, in truth, the trend reflects little more than the discipline that an analyst can impose, much aided by imagination.

Contrary to appearances, this monograph is not hostile to trend projection; indeed, how could it be? How could we seek to anticipate the future prudently if we were to eschew trend spotting? The prudent attitude to adopt towards trend projection has to be one of skepticism. My reason is overwhelmingly empirical. To be specific, the record of U.S. trend projection, and that of everyone else, has been abysmally poor.[11] More to the point, it is relatively easy to understand why this has been so. The problem has been the insoluble one of impossibility. Individual genius, strength of motivation, and official institutional backing, cannot reveal what is hidden by the very nature of the course of future strategic history. The dynamism of adversarial creativity, the scope for human discretionary behavior, and the irregular intervention of contingency, have been more than capable of frustrating the pretensions to advance knowledge of the future. But, I recognize that there is compulsion to attempt the impossible. Cynically, perhaps, one should note that distant trend projection is politically relatively safe. Contemporary authors of such projection will be highly unlikely to remain in positions wherein they may face punishment for their more obvious errors of judgment. It is probably relevant to observe that trend projection offers some protection from the sheer scale of the data hypothesized as potential evidence for the chosen guesswork. Whereas the anticipation of an individual event, a prediction or forecast, will be lonely in its uniqueness, trend projection can fight on even if damaged by the nonoccurrence of what is claimed should be expected. There are several good reasons why social science, whatever its virtues, is not science (testable for reliability), but it has the utility to its practitioners of being able to condone failures as tolerable exceptions to general rules.[12]

    c. Defense analysis. The final topic in this review of educated futurology is defense analysis, understood here as meaning the typically mathematically shaped and driven analysis of choices in defense preparation for the future. Defense analysis frequently is mistaken for defense planning, just as contingency (including war) planning for the production of discrete plans is assumed not unreasonably to be the planners' output. Defense planning in its meaning for this monograph refers to purposeful preparation for defense of the country's national security in the future. Defense analysis, metric or qualitative, can contribute little to the subject here. Although such analysis feeds debate and may ease decision with respect to the "ways" and "ends" of strategy, its very nature generally restricts its domain of proper concern to the "means" element in the strategy triptych. This is not to deny that calculation of "means" can and should influence policy and strategy, but such calculation is always likely to be bounded by choices already made politically and expressed strategically. Broadly subcategorized, there are two kinds of defense analysis; operations research and systems analysis. The former matured exponentially as practical, but scientific advice about known elements in support of military action; while the latter emerged and then matured a generation later, finally achieving bureaucratic ascendancy in the era of Pentagon management led forcefully by Robert S. McNamara. Systems analysis is a basket of typically mathematical methods designed to enable, certainty to facilitate, the making of important choices among competing solutions to defense problems.[13] The generally worthy purpose of this defense analysis was to enable discovery and testing of scientifically correct answers to pressing problems. Both in fact and legend, scientific defense analysis was compared and contrasted with the allegedly intuitive wisdom of military experience expressed largely in a qualitative mode.[14] McNamara's reign in the Pentagon, by necessity, obliged senior uniformed opponents of official civilian preferences to join the ranks of the metrically competent. This is now old history, though it did leave a legacy of military resentment, as well as a far more numerate culture significant in the making of defense decisions.

For the particular purpose of this monograph, the most important quality worthy of serious note about numerate defense analysis is its limited relevance. For a while, America's principal allies were overimpressed by the McNamara revolution, feeling as analytically inadequate for competition with the civilian "whiz-kids" as originally were America's armed services. However, the realization slowly dawned that, important though it was to be able to design and conduct cost-benefit analyses, and to generate testably and therefore allegedly provably reliably correct (i.e., scientifically verifiable) answers, this group of methods could not address, let alone seek to answer, the questions for future defense planning that must matter most. Bluntly stated, the mathematics did not work, because it could not analyze the more important problems. This is not to be critical of defense analysis, either in the form of systems analysis or of operations research. These analytical methods require certainty of data before they can endeavor to productively yield reliable certainty in answers. But, when one strives to prepare future defense for national security, one soon discovers that there are few certainties that could be pressed into metric service for the generation of reliably correct scientific answers. Numerate defense analysis can be of high value to the country only when it is assigned tasks that have authority from outside such analysis, and which the analysis itself cannot possibly provide. For an obvious generic example: defense analytical methodology may be able to determine the respective cost-effectiveness of several alternative strategic nuclear force postures, but such analyses are only helpful if you first have knowledge of the adversary's decision-making, and his values as well as our own: a strategic balance is not conveniently self-interpreting in meaning for our security.

One discovers that future defense planning simply cannot be founded upon a basis of objectively reliable scientific knowledge, regardless of the integrity and skill of our defense analysts. The reason, of course, is that these dedicated professionals cannot know the unknowable. This means, quite unavoidably, that we cannot determine our future defense needs with any aspiration to achieve reliable certainty. Zealous pursuit of certainty of knowledge through defense analysis is a chimera. There is much that such analysis can demonstrate, provided the relevant parameters are known. Not only should we recognize that international relations are not governed by professional defense analysis, in addition we need to take on board

13

fully Carl von Clausewitz's argument about war's adversarial nature in a context characterized by incentives to make discretionary choices.

For defense analysis to demonstrate its worth, the country first must decide whether, what, when, where, and how, it may like to exercise an option for military action. Once these questions are answered well enough, defense analysis advantageously can address the "how" and "with what" issues of most suitable military ways and means to achieve the desired political and strategic effectiveness. The bottom line on defense analysis has to be that it must depend for its utility on elements beyond its disciplinary boundary. Specifically: judgments most relevant to future national security flow as a consequence of politics, human discretion, culture, and sheer contingency. Defense analysis may have influence on and for any, or indeed all, of these, but there is no sensible way in which one can conduct defense planning without taking comprehensive note of the multiple sources of uncertainty. Much as lawyers are wont to seek to reduce national defense to a set of legal challenges, and ethicists see defense (and war) primarily through a moral lens, so metrically competent defense analysts can have difficulty appreciating the limits to the utility of mathematics. Strategic history has provided many examples of the wrong wars being waged with considerable technical skill. Studies of cost-effectiveness should attend very carefully indeed to the desirability of the political and strategic effectiveness that may well be achievable at tolerable cost. For an obvious example, there was much that the U.S. Army did well in and about South Vietnam; the problem was the shortage of political and strategic sense in the whole mission.[15]

(1) **Humanities**. Disciplines properly categorized as an art in the context of this monograph are the ones that can be useful in educating for adequate performance on and across the "strategy bridge."[16] Three disciplines in particular need to be regarded as a *gestalt* that should be capable of serving to educate those who must attempt to grapple with the issues of policy and strategy that concern the higher reaches of defense planning. The three arts most directly in focus here are politics, strategy, and history. Comprehension of these disciplines yields first-order understanding of the issues that one can be confident will arise in the future in need of alleviation, if not solution. The approach flagged above as "educated futurology" is of direct value principally, indeed overwhelmingly, only to the meeting of second-order challenges. To clarify, American decisions in the future on issues requiring policy guidance will be resolved politically and must be in need of strategy. There is variably extant an impressive empirical historical record of political and strategic experience that can be tapped with care for understanding of pertinent behavior. By way of sharp contrast to the contributions from arts disciplines, science and social science do not offer methodologies useful for the derivation of helpful understanding of the strategic future.[17]

The inherent strength of science is its requirement for testably repeatable proof of hypotheses. It yields certainty of knowledge that is reliable; if it does not, it cannot be science. Social science seeking to be useful for the understanding of future strategic history necessarily and unarguably has to be naked of any direct data that might be theorized as evidence privileging particular interpretations of events yet to occur. When social science seeks to proceed both from and with the past into the future, it discovers—at least it should do so—that specific historical prediction is mission impossible. While there is everything to be said in favor of the mobilization of historical understanding for the purpose of educating contemporary defense planning, prediction of potentially vital particulars, the details, must always be systemically unsound. In other words, the enduring dynamism in the nature of policy and strategic decisions precludes reliability as to their prediction. This is not simply an argument in an open debate; rather is it a fact the truth of which is as readily illustrated as it is easily explained.[18]

The subject here is dominated by the certain knowledge that, in the future, human beings with free will acting with discretion in competition with other human beings, motivated with variable potency by elements accommodated in the Thucydidean triptych, must manage all the hazards and opportunities of contingency—known, unknown and unknowable.[19] The distinguished historian, Michael Howard, has ventured the judgment that social scientists need to be modest in any aspirations they may entertain in order to be able to predict the future. He commented as follows:

> But in formulating laws that will be either predictive or normative social scientists have been no more successful than historians; for the number of variables is so incalculable, the data inevitably so incomplete. The theories they formulate are at best explanatory or heuristic. They can never be predictive. Even the most convincing of their theories should be regarded as tentative hypotheses to be critically re-examined as new data becomes available.[20]

Howard is damning in his denial of predictive wisdom as a realistic expectation for social science, but I suggest that his case could have been stated even more strongly. Specifically, even if we could identify all of the variables relevant to strategic history, the factors of discretionary license and contingency, especially in the adversarial context for creative thought and behavior, must frustrate the ambition to predict with the confidence of certainty. I find that the challenge of selecting methodology suitable for a subject with the nature of future strategic history, by plausible analogy at least, was addressed very directly by Clausewitz with respect to future war. He composed the following advice, in words that remain widely and justly admired:

> The first, the supreme, the most far-reaching act of judgment that the statesman and commander have to make is to establish by that test [of fit with policy] the kind of war on which they are embarking: neither mistaking it for, nor trying to turn it into, something that is alien to its nature. That is the first of all strategic questions and the most comprehensive.[21]

My claim for analogy pertains to the nature of strategic history in the future and the impossibility of seeking to examine it usefully by means of methods that are thoroughly disabled, not merely disadvantaged, by their nature. Simply to ask the basic question, "Who and what will make future American strategic history?" really is to answer it with an all but deafening admission of unavoidable ignorance—at least with respect to specific detail identifiable with predictive certainty.

To be positive, however, there are grounds for high confidence in our understanding of the principal influences, forces perhaps, that will determine whether the great stream of time will flow strategically in the future. Although assuredly we cannot predict the future in detail, we do know the major reasons why it should follow a particular course. No less helpfully, we enjoy access, in useful and usable detail, to the strategic history of much in the past and present. Inexorably, this monograph is heading towards the difficult ground of analogy and the perils of dangerous anachronism. Central to this monograph is the assumption that strategic history in the future will resemble past and present strategic history in critically important respects.[22] If this is believed by readers to be an assumption too far, then this whole analysis and the illustrative detail offered below, must fail to persuade.

As Harold Lasswell argued, "The study of politics is the study of influence and the influential."[23] Regarded analytically, politics is free of all content save for that arguably all important quality, influence — which is power (an even more heavily contested concept). Across time, space, and cultures, the permanent goal in politics and of politicians is always influence. This inherently relational variable is, and has to be, a currency with value common to any and all issues in contemporary debate. It is as certain as anything can be about the human estate that future strategic history will be political in nature. The struggle to secure more influence, in order both to secure more control with preferred content over the external world, and for the simple joy of being more influential/powerful, is permanent. Strategically regarded, the future will see political ends pursued with variable skill, vigor, and physical capability, by the sovereign (and semi-sovereign) polities that must make history. We do not know and cannot divine exactly which issues between polities will fuel political action most energetically, but we do know for certain that those issues will be discovered or invented and exploited. It is important to recognize the reality that the quality of political issues in normative terms (assessed when, and by whom) essentially has to be regarded as irrelevant to this analysis. No matter what the moral tone and content may be in the years to come of strategic history, the management of particular issues must always be political: that is to say, people and their polities will have to seek influence if they are to be influential – and this requires political process. I have ventured this somewhat basic explanation of why politics is what it is and why it endures, because the focus here requires utmost clarity upon the matter. If one were uncertain, even confused, about future strategic history, then prudent American preparation for it could be needlessly challenging. In illustration, it might be believed by some unrealistic optimists among us that the American eagle, the Chinese dragon, and the Russian bear, might be able to co-exist cooperatively in general amity out into the distant future. This author approves of such a notion but is obliged by his understanding of the past and the present to be skeptical. Moreover, if the human future is no less political than it was in the past or is in the present, there can be no plausible basis upon which one could reasonably found a theory that in effect would write the demise of political thought and behavior.

It is simply human to be political. Unfortunately, but unavoidably, being human and seeking influence through political process means that one is caught by the consequences of the commanding emotional and intellectual logic in Thucydides' eternal and ubiquitous triptych of fear, honor, and interest. This may read like a rather hard-nosed variant of "Civics 101," but what I have just described is the bare, but essential and unavoidable, architecture of American security (and insecurity) in the future. Bears and dragons cannot help being influence-seeking beasts. Considering ourselves strategically, as prudently we must, we cannot, indeed dare not, be significantly different.[24]

The discussion immediately above has sought to deconstruct the political ends in the strategy trinity in search of the fuel for human history—past, present, and prospective future. If Thucydides holds true for the future, as I believe, and for the reason of enduring political motivation, then we can be sufficiently confident in employing the past in our endeavor to locate understanding useful for efforts to educate for prudent defense planning today. Of course, acute dangers lurk to trap the unwary in careless misuse of strategic history. The most substantial peril probably lies in the abuse of analogy. Lest there should be any misunderstanding in this regard, I must emphasize my suspicion of analogy and, indeed, my disdain for it. If history should repeat itself in detail in the future, it will not be for anticipated reasons in which high confidence should have been placed. There are always likely to be a few, a very few, people who do guess correctly in particular detail about the future. But, there can never be a reliable way of knowing at the time who they are. Proof positive of predictive sagacity may well be provable in and after the event, but only—unhelpfully—with the sublime benefit of retrospective knowledge.

Ironically, perhaps, given the analysis immediately above, the next section of this monograph may be characterized as an exercise in analogy on a large scale, though such a view would be only half correct, at most. I intend to identify what it is that we can and should learn from history. This is not to claim that "History teaches lessons." History does nothing of the sort, it is absent in the past that is gone. However, that record of thought and behavior over the course of 2 1/2 millennia does lend itself to interpretation that appears plausibly capable of serving as good enough empirical grounds for anticipation of our strategic future. What I am attempting is strategic historical analogy, typically on a grand scale, that should allow anticipation on our part. This will not and cannot be a foolish exercise in attempted predictive analogy. The egregious folly of such an effort should be in no further need of highlighting here. On the off chance that any reader remains in doubt on the point, argument by historical analogy regarding specific future events is completely impossible because we cannot know exactly which events will occur. It has to follow, logically, that we are unable to pick a winner among candidate analyses of the past. However, once we elevate our sights from particular events with their granular detail, we discover many similarities that recur across time, geography, and culture. One should not be fooled by the gladius and hob-nailed sandals of a legionary into assuming that his circumstances were *sui generis*. The Romans and Carthaginians, who probably between them suffered more than 80,000 fatalities on a single day in 216 BC at Cannae in southern Italy, had much that looks to be common strategically, operationally, and tactically, with our soldiers in modern times. By this, I mean that our contemporary ideas of strategy, operation, and tactics, enable us carefully to make sense of what happened in the Second Punic War. Howard was not disrespectful of the past when he claimed that the wars throughout history have had more in common with each other than they have with other categories of human behavior in their own particular context of time, place, and culture.[25]

I have argued thus far that because the laws of nature prevent us from penetrating the specific mysteries of future strategic history with any scientific (or social-scientific) assurance, we are obliged to attempt to employ past experience (the stories woven by historians as "History") as a guide in aid of our education for future defense planning. There is much reassurance to be found in recognition that this cannot be an exercise in particular analogy. Unlike some military theorists of early modern times, we will not recommend re-creation of the Roman legion, which already was a lost cause when Vegetius made the despairing attempt in his writing at the very end of the 4th century AD, let alone in late-15th century Europe.[26] However, the combat discipline of the Roman legions, and the rigorous training essential for it, have echoes that still speak eloquently to us today.

For this monograph to have some utility to the U.S. Army, it is necessary for it to be focused on matters in which most contemporary soldiers typically will not be expert. It so happens that the tactical, logistical, and technological issues on which our soldiers are indeed well-prepared, are exactly those issues that, by and large in specific detail, can have few, if any, valuable echoes over decades and centuries. Attempts to look analogically at future strategic history through what would be tactical or even operational lenses from the past must be close to absurd. The result would be an analysis wherein anachronism would run riot. Instead, the challenge for the next section is to identify what we should be able to learn from strategic history without, as a necessary consequence, affronting the laws of physics or common sense.

What Can We Learn From Strategic History?

This section advances claims that are explained not in the spirit of "lessons," but rather as explanations of phenomena presented as general truths relevant to the role and performance of the U.S. Army.

1. Military motivation: why some armies fight much better than others. There is no simple formula that can serve to explain fighting power with unchallengeable authority. That said, fighting power in combat proficiency can be studied in exemplars through the ages. It is plausible to argue that armies reflect the leading qualities in the societies from which they are recruited. Since our society is what it is and for a while has to be, this is not a very helpful insight, true though it probably is. More helpful is the knowledge that the better fighting forces throughout history have been characterized by combat discipline, by confidence in military leadership, and by flexibility and openness to needed adaptations in the real-time of combat experience in the field.[27] Given that extraordinary competence, let alone genius, is not, has never been, and cannot be the norm among generals, plainly combat success often has owed much, if not most, to leadership at the tactical level, as well as to the fortunate fact of enemy incompetence. It may be morally sound as well as empirically arguably accurate, to argue that generals command the armies they deserve, and similarly soldiers are led by the generals they deserve. Nonetheless, although armies have been let down by incompetent commanders, and some generals, in effect, have been betrayed by a weak soldiery, it appears to be true to claim that generals and their soldiers tend to reinforce each other's strengths and/or weaknesses. The data of experience that is evidence is unremarkably fairly steady on this critically important subject. There is no reason to anticipate that this subject will be altered by parametric changes anytime soon. If the essence of war is battle, its climate is unchanging as one which in its enduring nature is characterized by "danger, exertion, uncertainty, and chance."[28] Warfare is changing tactically all the time, but there are good reasons to be confident that its human element will remain critically essential. The automation of some combat activity is not likely to abolish the necessity for boots on the ground, save in exceptional circumstances. The goal of political control of ground and those who live on the ground, is as old as strategic history.[29] There continue to be limits to the strategic and political effectiveness of threats and actions from distance. Notwithstanding the technical wonders of contemporary (and anticipatable future) body armor and combat medicine, we can alas be highly confident in the expectation that combat will remain hazardous to one's physical well-being. Experience over centuries has demonstrated that willingness, if not necessarily eagerness, to fight at the extreme risk of one's life is a function very much of a vital sense of loyalty, inclusively understood. Moreover, most commonly it is a loyalty strongly felt to immediate elements: comrades, unit, possibly regiment, and particular relatively junior leaders. Other loyalties also figure: to family, tribe, clan, and nation, for example. But, the loyalty to comrades caught in the command dilemmas of survival in combat tend to be dominant. Great distant abstractions of belief tend only to be background factors, when considered in light of the necessities of "now." Of course, individual motivation is typically somewhat subject to group pressures to conform, even in extremely dangerous behaviors. Discipline and training, with the two intertwined as mutually dependent, can offset some lack of the "moral fiber" that may afflict relatively unwilling soldiers, though experience has shown that there is a pragmatic discipline of dire circumstance, sometimes capable of compensating for what God may have neglected to provide in the necessary quantity.

2. Training: superior training regimes are not entirely reliable as keys to victory. Although rigorous training should always be a vital contributor to fighting power, one must never forget that war is an activity that is in its very nature adversarial. This means that I could not add as a supplementary comment the beckoning thought, "but they always help," to the title of this comment. The reason is because training that appears superior, may in fact only be training against a notional enemy who is assumed to behave in tolerably cooperative ways, albeit in attempted belligerent competition. The French Army in the late 1930s probably was trained adequately, if barely, for its dominant task of operating from behind the Maginot Line, which was—perhaps one should say would have been—impregnable to assault. Unfortunately, the Line was only impregnable to the ways and means of warfare of 1918.[30] Training, no matter how admirably rigorous, is always in principle at risk to enemies able to behave in a manner with which the authoritative doctrine behind the training cannot cope.[31] The French (and British) disaster in Flanders in 1940 was a text book example of the fatal problem for training with inappropriate doctrine. Notwithstanding the strong caveat just aired, military history reveals the general truth in this second point. Aside from the technical competence that sound training imparts, that training is a crucial source of self-confidence for soldiers, both the tactically led and the tactical leaders. When, perhaps if, creative inspiration in generalship is missing from the action, an army well trained for competent tactical performance can provide some useful compensation for what is absent from its higher direction.

3. Experience and expertise: military experts in peacetime are not to be trusted (entirely!) As rookie quarterbacks learn on the first game day of the regular National Football League season, there is no reliable and adequate substitute for the real thing. Actual warfare, combat, is unlike any other experience in the human record. Also, for a relatively constructive point, the unique qualities attendent upon warfare effectively have been constant through the ages.[32] This is an important reason why we can be somewhat confident concerning an understanding of war in the future that must rest upon our comprehension of its actuality in the past and present. Although armies are defined most essentially as institutions prepared for the possibility of war—that is what they are for, expressed with reference to the most basic function— actual warfare is such a unique set of behaviors that no preparation in peacetime can achieve more than a rough approximation of real combat experience. No matter how realistically drills and exercises are designed and conducted to be, the reality always comes as a shock to expectations forged and matured in and by peacetime. This is one of the reasons why soldiers and scholars emphasize flexibility and adaptability as vitally important. There is a need to be flexible and adaptable for suitably creative behavior in the face of a like creative and probably innovative enemy. In addition, all armies (and navies and air forces) need to be capable of shifting gears radically in order to cope instantly and personally with the trials of actual warfare, meaning violence at its most extreme. It should not be forgotten that, although there have been many periods wherein armies waged war after war *seriatim* in relatively short temporal order, the default circumstance very often has been one wherein war had not been experienced recently, and was not anticipated for the near future. As a special, indeed a truly unique, historical case, consider the experience of the U.S. Strategic Air Command (SAC) from 1946 until the demise of the Soviet adversary at the end of 1991.[33] Through all of those years SAC needed to be ready, which is to say really ready, for war, and yet not so ready that it might itself inadvertently trigger World War III. The Command did not spare itself in the demands made upon its people and machines for a sufficiency-plus of motivation to fight. But it would be difficult to exaggerate the inherent contradictory tensions between readiness and safety, maintained improbably but literally for decades. Notwithstanding a small library of technical studies of anticipated and possibly believed probable wartime and post-war conditions, SAC could not know what nuclear warfare, almost certainly bilateral, would really be like, other than incalculably awful. The critical issue of institutional and military morale, of contingent motivation, is almost beyond comprehension. Happily, the long remaining hypothetical nuclear World War III provided an historically exceptional example of military forces required literally to be combat ready over many years on next to no notice. Whether or not SAC could have shifted smoothly into the unknowns of Defense Condition (DEFCON) 1, we do not know, but we do know for certain that no army, bar none, has ever been completely ready for the actual experience of warfare. Politicians have not always understood that armies most typically do not experience for real their most essential *raison d'etre*. Indeed, as Howard has commented wryly, the maintenance of an army in peacetime can be so demanding a task that one is apt to forget what an army is for.[34] That most defining of functions is combat, battle, and it is a unique experience admitting of no convincingly close substitutes.[35] The challenge to try and anticipate an enemy's creative behavior in a war that must be unique in critical respects, is a demand that we are near certain to fail to meet with full adequacy. We are never sufficiently ready for war and its warfare, notwithstanding official assurances to the contrary.

4. Brain, skill, and muscle: wars are won by the ways in which weapons are used. It is a commonplace error to claim that particular weapons won a war; popular TV programs on military history especially are prone to commit this fundamental error. The proper characterization ought always to be "the weapons with which the war was won." The past and present record of warfare of all kinds demonstrates clearly that although the weapon certainly is important, the skill and determination with which it is wielded matter much more. The understanding of how to employ a weapon always needs application in different contexts: individual, joint in combined arms, and en masse by tactical and operational direction or generalship. Individual lethality is important in most cases, but warfare is typically a social activity conducted by large numbers of agents. It is probably true to argue that technology engineered into weaponry has been the principal shaper and even driver of tactical innovation in history.[36] However, similar technological access among belligerents has not invariably led to commonality of engineering or tactical choice. One needs to beware of succumbing too easily to the attraction of the idea of technological determinism. It is not always the case that a superior tactical use for a weapon, with a subsequent dominant operational preference, will be demonstrated, let alone be demonstrable. Not infrequently, weapons could lend themselves to alternative tactical uses, which might have profoundly alternative operational meaning. The point requiring registration is that the strategist's eternal question, "So what?" must be asked of all weaponry, past, present, and prospectively future. A weapon is only a military tool in tactical application, developed ultimately for its strategic and its political merit in effectiveness. Every weapon throughout history has required understanding of its value individually, but almost always for the conduct of combined arms. The excitement of technological novelty and, in recent times, photogenic attractiveness have served to discourage a due quality of strategic thought about material change. Most recently, our present-day military experience with computers has been a distinctly strategy-light happening.[37] That said, there is no reason for substantial doubt that our future strategic history will see us groping in the dark, as always has been more or less the case. Fundamentally, the challenge for the future must be the same as in the past. Specifically, an understanding of how new weapons can be employed most effectively is only learned reliably by experience in war. Tactical ideas about weapon use, and operational grasp concerning the exploitation of tactical effectiveness, more usually follow, rather than precede, combat. In addition, one should never forget the adversarial and contingent qualities central to war and its warfare. A strategically and operationally innovative yet competent enemy, especially if he is fortunate in his choices

(guesses), can more than offset sound-seeming ortho-
dox views in our current military doctrine.

**5. Competence in command: high competence
cannot prudently be assumed to be a normal condition of military leadership**. This claim sounds damning, which indeed it is, but it needs contextualization
for a fair and balanced view. To begin with the obvious, most episodes of warfare over millennia have
recorded verdicts that identified winners and losers
unambiguously, if sometimes "on points" rather than
conclusively. Even if defeated generals played a los-
ing hand in battle as well as reasonably should have
been anticipated, there is no denying that coming in
plainly second in the most defining feature of strategic history, which is to say battle, is likely to be some
testimony as to the rival competencies in generalship
demonstrated. The limitations of particular individuals as generals can be critically important, but for my
purpose here it is necessary to flag the extraordinary
contextual problems inescapable from the burdens
of higher military command. The strategic history of
belligerents in any period quickly reveals the truly
exceptional demands made of generalship by the nature and the character of the command and leadership
tasks. To summarize what would be an extensive list
of typical challenges, the general must both command
and lead his army in all its articulated parts for the
benefit of strategy which he may influence, but fundamentally that he did not invent and design; pursue
his operational plan flexibly and adaptively in the face
of the enemy (who must be assumed to be adaptive
and competent); meet contingencies of all kinds both
calmly yet often, of necessity, creatively; and last but
not least, never forget that the warfare he is waging is
only about the political ends that should be the reward

for military advantage.[38] The strategic history of all periods, past and present, records circumstances for the exercise of generalship that could not fail to make extraordinary demands upon both individuals and their immediate supporting institutions, challenges that were close to being unreasonable makes no difference. A frequent mistake is made today when the complexities of contemporary war and warfare are compared and allegedly contrasted with the apparent simplicity of times long past. This belief typically is nonsense. A little empathy for the whole context of ancient and medieval war soon reveals sets of problems quite as troublesome as are those of today: they were different, but also they were the same as are those that tend to frustrate us today. Modern medicine, computers, jet aircraft, and the rest of the contemporary scene, have only relegated long-past military experience in terms of its detail. The problems have been shifted by social, political, and technological change, but the difficulties of high command have not eased meaningfully, and they never will.

An important sub-text to this fifth point is the fact that because strategic history per se does not have a "story arc," it can have no final moves. We can be certain that our strategic future will be as harassed by difficulties that challenge our future generals' competence, as was our strategic past. The American defense community, inclusively comprehended, comprises a talented collectivity of would-be problem solvers. Moreover, our political, military, administrative, and technological problem solvers frequently will succeed in their tasks for now. But, problems of like difficulty will hinder strategic performance in the future, for certain, because it is in the very nature of the enterprise of defense planning against uncertain foes in unknown circumstances that this has to be so. There will never be a pivot point in American strategic history, beyond which will lie only broad sunlit uplands of security unchallenged by menaces on or over the temporal horizon of the day. Once this grip upon the inalienable reality of strategic history is achieved, the educational value of its study should be considerably clarified for the benefit of skeptics.

6. Landpower: ground and people. We learn from strategic history that, although war can be waged for many reasons and in a wide variety of ways, terrestrial, indeed territorial, reference has been a constant. The acquisition of political and possibly legal title to land by means of the violent coercion of organized force, currently is out of fashion in statecraft for most polities, but that contemporary fact, if it is a fact, is only recent and cannot be assumed to be permanent. Geopolitically generally "satisfied" societies and their states are wont to forget that territorial self-satisfaction is not a reliably enduring condition for most of mankind. Well within living memory, lust for territorial acquisition has been a major motivator for war. In order to help fuel our understanding of armed conflict in the 21st century, it is not necessary to attempt the impossible and seek to identify exactly who may strive to dominate whom by the threat or use of force. It is sufficient for us to know that Thucydides has been proven to be right by the strategic historical experience of 2 1/2 millennia. His triptych of fear, honor, and interest is all too plausibly adequate in the inclusivity of its capture of the principal motives in statecraft and war.[39] With high assurance we know that those mutually reinforcing political motives will continue to have territorial reference: three most essential constants in this monograph—humanity itself, political process, and strategy function—require it. Recognition of this enduring actuality has profound meaning for future defense planning.[40] American Landpower, most especially its ground power, must always be relevant to conflict, because of the nature of the American strategic condition. Our humanity restricts us to territorial residency, and effectively the whole world comprises a physical geography for which political, and legally (albeit sometimes contested) sovereign title is owned or claimed. Even when territory itself is not in contention as a major issue, there is a permanency in the nature of war that commands relevancy for our land (and ground) power. While warfare will be conducted in five geographically distinct (if most typically joint, in practice) domains in the future, there is powerful reason to anticipate historical continuity in the superior effectiveness achievable by the expectation or reality of local presence on the ground.

The conduct of warfare is changing, and it has to be assumed that it will continue to do so. However, the reasons for the relatively superior potency of the threat or actuality of local American presence on the ground are well-rooted in factors critical to the human condition. These factors are not merely expedient for a preferred character of contemporary warfare. The importance of the U.S. Army in the future is underwritten by the necessary territorial nature of man's estate, and by human behavior that has to be both political and strategic. The ground-power narrative in U.S. national security in the 21st century thus is founded upon our understanding of actualities that must persist. Strategic competition in defense plans from the extra-territorial domains of military power is both real and, regarded jointly as it must be, to be welcomed as generally complementary. On occasion, the U.S. Government will see strategic advantage in employing sea power, air power, space power, and now cyber power, as partial or wholesale substitutes for ground power. Such a preference, though understandable when deep commitment is not wanted, comes with district limitations that are the unavoidable costs of the anticipated benefits. Fly-by strikes from altitude will always be attractive, as will be the chaos that may be wrought by cyber offense. However, neither will be able to attain the kind of control over adversary behavior that uniquely is to be secured by Wylie's "man on the scene with a gun."[41] It should be needless for this monograph to recognize explicitly the episodic fact that the control desired over people on the ground quite often is not secured. But that persisting fragility about the case for the threat and use of armed force is an enduring problem for politics and strategy, rather than for the army itself. Warfare is always brutal and should only be conducted for well understood and politically managed strategic reasons.

7. **War and warfare: every war is unique, yet familiar**. Provided the concept of war is defined and explained with ironic liberality, it is not hard to understand why it has endured across time, space, and culture. The contemporary defense planner in search of some understanding that could have educational value is spoiled for choice by the dreadful richness of our strategic historical experience. Once the barrier to ready appreciation effected by unfamiliar detail about almost everything is passed, enlightenment should begin to shine. Initially skeptical students can hardly help but notice that the historical experience of strategy is only really anachronistic if they regard the subject with an undisciplined ethnocentricity.[42] The differences between "then" in the past, virtually

any past, and "now," let alone the future, should be unneeded and therefore unworthy of much comment. But sensibly, if one is equipped with theory that adequately orders and explains human behavior, political process, and strategy—and we are so equipped—then one can find a common transhistorical meaning in, say, Greek, Roman, Norman, or any medieval and modern episodes that bear much strategic historical weight. Strategy and stratagem as we comprehend them today were as alive and as useful in the Second Punic War of the 3rd century BC, as they were in the protracted Anglo–French struggles in the 14th and 15th, and the 18th and early-19th centuries AD.[43] So long as one does not become distracted by strategic behavior and misbehavior that ought unquestionably to be categorized as thoroughly unfit for time travel, every level of strategic performance, from battlefield tactics up to and including grand strategy, can have some relevance for today and tomorrow. This is not, at best it should not be, a vulgar presentism. If we explore and examine strategic behavior functionally by category, the common sense in this approach to understanding is all but obvious. Nothing important in strategic history has changed with time, when the details are appreciated by category.

To illustrate my argument: civil-military relations have varied very extensively with time, place, and culture, but the importance of the relationship between military power and political influence has endured. For another case with pervasive and enduring importance, logistics have altered mightily in all aspects of detail over the centuries, but for 2 1/2 millennia they have remained matters of unchanging necessity. Once one has unwrapped much of the period detail—from any period—one discovers that this critically significant subject has not really altered. Issues of supply and movement were as important to Alexander the Great as they have been to his U.S. and North Atlantic Treaty Organization (NATO) successors in what now is known as Afghanistan.[44]

If one can escape from a presentist cocoon on matters of detail that do not travel temporally, one discovers that there are few, if any, current or anticipatably possible future strategic challenges of kinds that have not troubled strategists in the past. Of course, all problems are, in detail, characteristic of their time and place, but when regarded functionally, they will appear in approximate categories of concern that are timeless. I must hasten to admit that grave problems in one period (for example, health and medical knowledge) can fade to a distinctly tolerable level in a later time.[45] It is not suggested here that problem-sets have proved constant in intensity from period to period, only that categories of issues with strategic meaning have tended strongly to persist as subjects of concern through time.

The would-be futurological defense planner can learn from strategic history that: surprise of several kinds always happens; chance can rule in war and reduce meticulously planned ventures to a condition of chaos; Clausewitz's compound concept of "friction" will be ever present at every level of behavior and misbehavior in the future;[46] and that the concept of an impossible task does have meaning even, dare I say it, if one is an American Soldier. Leaning forward with some intellectual confidence, the strategist will have learned from the entire record of strategic history that episodes of war and of peace succeed each other in cyclical fashion. Indeed, this has been so marked a feature of strategic history, that one is tempted to frame as a hypothesis the idea that there is a necessary combination of causes in peace and in war for each condition to require its succession by the other. The succession has been highly irregular temporally, but its persistence is undeniable. Naturally, this provides no proof as to the character of future strategic history. However, it certainly should serve to discourage deep optimism. That war is a terrible affliction for a society is not a great revelation. The tactical horrors of combat, as well as its side-effects and consequences, were as well known to the Greeks and the Romans as they are to us today. This is not a truth we are in need of learning.

8. Politics and strategy: why and how strategic history "works." A common weakness among defense professionals is an undue reluctance to accept the fact of the sovereign authority of politics. Military and strategic advice is always hostage to political preference and discretion. The past and the present of our strategic history attest abundantly to the persisting truth in this claim. Regardless of the form of contemporary governance, political authority will command military action, for good, ill, or both. All but invariably, effectively licensed military experts find an official audience accepting of their recommendations only when the technical advice is tolerably in accord with the perceived political will of the relevant security community. It might be supposed that the leadership function of top-most political authority contradicts the argument just made. After all, cannot and do not leaders decide whither the community should be led? In practice, the universal and eternal historical reality that is the phenomenon of political leadership Is empirical testament to leaders' practical and prudent appreciation of the vital importance of political support that is legitimizing. Leaders in any age, culture, or political system, must enjoy the politically enabling quality of public consent.

The important point here is the need to appreciate that political consent, even if it is only a somewhat fearful toleration, is a permanent requirement for strategic behavior in times of both peace and war. Because of their military expertise, it is a challenge for strategic experts to take fully on board the fact that politics is an activity utterly devoid of subject-specific content, beyond that pertaining to the all-important struggle to be influential, or at least to influence those who are so. Politics, in its nature, is not about anything in particular beyond influence over other people.[47] To this end, people's values are translated into policy arguments and suggestions. It follows as a logical necessity that future national security cannot usefully be advanced unless one is able to translate one's expert strategic understanding into the political currency of helpful assistance to those who are or would-be influential. Political expertise means expertise in the art of becoming and being influential; it is radically different in kind from the expertise of, for example, brain surgery. This is not to suggest that aspiring politicians are indifferent to policy content, indeed, they are obliged of necessity to seek public legitimacy by promises to privilege some values over others. Nonetheless, it is only prudent to be willing to learn from the strategic history of ourselves and of others that, although "politics rules," it need not rule wisely. Political leadership, strictly understood, means leadership by those who have succeeded in being influential over others, period.

It is probably impossible to overstate the relative importance of political judgment to future national security. This is why the argument developed immediately above is so significant. The fundamental requirement for political leadership in any system of governance in any period is only that the relevant public consents to be led. We learn from strategic history that political and strategic errors typically are far more damaging than are operational or tactical mistakes.[48] Even when operational and tactical level mistakes are corrected systemically, an unsound political and/or strategic framework is likely to render the corrections ultimately futile, no matter the authentic expertise based empirically and impeccably on recent experience in the field. Iraq and Afghanistan provide fairly plain evidence concerning the unfortunate consequences of faulty policy and strategy.

Because the pursuit of national security must be assumed to be a journey without end in the great stream of time, there is need to learn from history how to cope well enough with the sometimes rival challenges presented in anticipation of both near-term and far-term futures. The key problems are that both futures are more than marginally problematic. The near-term, which may mean tomorrow, if not later today, could be characterized by an utterly unanticipated "Black Swan" event, or at least by anticipated happenings that were not expected to occur for years to come.[49] The concept of the far-term (or at least further) future is plagued by the indiscipline of an absence of identifiable temporal boundaries. To reduce the arbitrary quality to analysis and planning, one may select from experience with like equipment some expected useful service lifetime estimates pertaining to major military items. Alternatively, one might simply accept some currently fashionable, but reasonable sounding, date in the future that unquestionably will transcend the temporal region governing most troubling contemporary concerns. However, adroit wording must not be allowed to hide the uncertainties that require some definite answers. Time has to be the dimension of strategy that is least forgiving of error. One may find compensating fixes for lead-time needed but imprudently lost, however as a general rule strategic history reveals that misuse of the blessings of peacetime tend to be punished in the field when the conflict cycle returns to a wartime setting. Politically fashionable strategic or astrategic ideas are reflected in untrained soldiers and equipment not developed, properly tested, or purchased in prudent quantity.

Strategic history provides ample proof of the prudence in strategic investment for the longer-term future, given that we anticipate with confidence that there will be no end to the necessity for national security. Scarcely less important, though, is the need to be ready enough to cope adequately with whatever the near-term future throws our way. There should be no misunderstanding of the political nature of this uncontentious argument. Decisions today mean lead-times for a "tomorrow" of variable duration, which inexorably must have the potential to influence our freedom of policy choice in the political arguments at particular times in the future.

We are obliged to try and learn from and with strategic history, in very good part because there is nothing else that can be mobilized usefully for the purpose of guidance in defense preparations for the future. There is great scope for discretion over what we choose to learn from history. It should not be controversial to observe that history, let alone "History" as the product of inadvertent reification, has no existential reality. The past is gone and cannot be retrieved as an active agent for the convenience of our contemporary education. In Howard's cautionary words, quoted earlier, "History is what historians write, and historians are part of the process they are writing about." In other words, in the constantly moving present, we decide what should be learned from the past, hopefully for the benefit of security in the future. In this monograph, I have sought to highlight both what can and what cannot be learned from study of the past, though the reasons for a guarded optimism are substantial. Ironically, perhaps it is the very abundance of helpful-seeming data that can work to subvert prudent judgment. The richness of historical data, the convenient presence in the past of evident continuities of human nature, political purpose, and the generic nature of strategic reasoning, all appear as a gigantic candy store ready enough for expedient exploitation by defense professionals today. The attractions are genuine and need to be recognized and operationalized. However, it is necessary not to be seduced by the fallacy of what one could term the reified abstract agent. A recent book made use of this fallacy when, in its title, it posed the question, *What Does History Teach?* The answer, of course, has to be a resounding "nothing!" The past is silent and departed; versions of its meaning are interpreted and told in the narratives of culturally subjective historians.[50]

The argument just made in objection to the "history teaches" theme may appear to be an unimportant example of irritating scholasticism. But, naturally I believe it is not. The proposition that "history teaches" unintentionally is subversive in two important respects, especially when using sound practise in our efforts to make use of strategic history. First, the claim that history educates or even sometimes instructs all but unavoidably accommodates mission creep in the legitimacy of asserted authority that it cannot merit. If we know anything for certain about strategic history in the stream of time, it is that every event is more or less unique in detail, and often in much more than detail. Second, it is necessary to strive for acceptance of the fact of anachronism in and about a past that is misapplied as an alleged play-book guide to the unknowable future. Such liberation helps vitally in enabling us to avoid the contextual capture that renders the historian unable to hack successfully his way through the forest of historically unique circumstance that can hinder or even deny the ability to find much meaning in "then" for "today" and "tomorrow."

To illustrate the argument just made, I will cite two very different subjects that many defense analysts would agree are likely to have a noteworthy future for good or ill in American strategic history: arms control, and counterinsurgency (COIN). These two episodically persisting subjects in strategic history have provided us with an abundance of empirical data for careful exploitation in the crafting of prudent explanatory theory. However, both categories of strategic behavior attracted fundamental conceptual errors that have contributed critically to the crafting of flawed policy and strategy. It is particularly apposite in the context of this discussion, because the historical record of both kinds of endeavor obviously merits authority over our understanding for the future. As a prediction, admittedly, the U.S. political system will choose not to learn what it could and should from its own strategic history in regard to these sets of issues.

To summarize, we know with high confidence that the modern theory of arms control is unsound, and its guidance of official practice is doomed to disappoint its American backers.[51] In addition, we have no difficulty explaining why this is so: it is no mystery. The founding paradox, more credibly the irony, of arms control is exactly and fatally wrong, notwithstanding its superficially attractive cleverness. Whereas the reality of political and therefore also military competition, is purported to require some cooperation in the mutual interest of mutual security, in practice strategic history does not work, indeed, has never worked, like that.[52] The inescapable reason for the frustration of this attractive theory is politics. Necessarily, and unavoidably, competing polities will continue to compete within the framework of arms control negotiations, in pursuit both of potentially useful strategic advantage and of denial of that advantage to a competitor. In short, arms control addresses the wrong problem. The difficulty is political not military; arms are only an instrument of political will. Repeatedly in the 20th century, disarmament or arms control agreements proved unsurprisingly to be negotiable when political relations were permissive, and impossible to achieve when they were not. Plainly, this is a case of politicians persistently declining to learn from what the evidence of history could only be interpreted to mean. However, this is not to be critical of political leaders. It is all too understandable why the general public tends to believe what it wants to believe, absent the undeniable imminence of dire peril. Political leaders are more than marginally hostage to the sentiments dominant in their electorates — and, up to an uncertain point, this is the way that governance should be.

COIN, my second case, also reveals a history of persistent, or at least repeated, political unwillingness to respect empirical knowledge of the past. For reasons of optimism founded on over-confidence, the United States in particular, but far from exclusively, has refused to learn from strategic history, including its own, that COIN efforts when led and generally dominated by nonindigenous military forces, cannot succeed. This argument is close to being a self-evident truism. It should be the show-preventing reason for the exercise of extreme political and strategic discretion whenever a local authority considers it's use as an aspirational exception to the well-attested rule. But the recent strategic history of Americans and others shows that both politicians and certain soldiers can resist well-attested facts until strategic history reveals yet again why enduring facts truly are that.[53] As with the arms control example explained above, no deep mystery confronts those who seek to explain what it is that conceals the path to success with COIN. Common sense and some historical reading should ignite understanding that foreign soldiers and officials typically do not enjoy and cannot speedily grasp the social, political and cultural differences of a foreign society required for success with COIN. Moreover, when and if we recognize this fact, such recognition is not synonymous with ability to meet the COIN problem. This is yet another case of strategic history presenting a challenge that it is impossible to meet, in this instance simply because "we" are who we are, and so also are "they." It is no disgrace to fail in attempts to achieve the difficult and demanding, but persistence in an effort to do the impossible is an affront to the Gods of strategy.

Conclusions and Recommendations.

This monograph concludes with five interdependent recommendations. It is not certain that these recommendations, alone or together, can resolve the problem of ensuring that defense preparations will, practically and effectively, meet the demands of future security. That granted, it is possible to make prudent preparation for future national security. The basis upon which such preparation can be founded is summarized in the five recommendations that follow:

1. Strategic History. This history of our strategic past and present is the sole empirical data base accessible to us that offers any real value for future national security. The Army should approach its task of preparing for the future by being suitably respectful of historical experience. This means in practice that, although there is very little, if anything, pertaining to future events that can or should be anticipated with high confidence, the situations in which the United States may well find itself will be anything but unprecedented in the history of America or other polities. The purpose of strategic historical study is not the spotting of analogies. There can be no analogies for a future that is unknowable at the level of detail. What is required is appreciation of the high educational value of history. A deeper understanding of our past is an excellent tool for training judgement and expanding imagination. The perils of inappropriate analogy and of anachronism can be difficult to avoid entirely, but education concerning the dangers should suffice to expose them. An historically well-educated officer corps soon will recognize unsound arguments that rely upon false or dubious analogy. The major point in need of firm reiteration is the inconvenient fact that the past (and arguably the present) is all that we have by way of an empirical, verifiable, understanding of strategic problems and their candidate solutions.

2. **Strategy**. There is some danger that education in the basic architecture of strategy may appear to license and even legitimize what could be a rather uncharacteristic approach to our subject. In short, one might use strategy's most essential elements—ends, ways and means—to instruct by adding a number of assumptions, only to find that one's approach was nearly all method at the intolerable cost of necessary content. That said, there is every reason to favor the respected triptych as the key that enables strategic performance, always provided political ends are treated with the care they should command. Strategy is never simply a matter of balancing tolerably well among ends, ways, and means, because the strategic ways chosen to employ available means can only make the necessary political sense if the policy ends are politically desirable. This does not diminish the utility of the discipline in the logic of strategy, because no policy end, regardless of its political sagacity, will be practicable if it is not enabled by strategy that guides the operational and tactical effectiveness of military assets. Professional historians have argued that our contemporary concept of strategy did not emerge unambiguously in any language until the 1770s. This is true. However, it is also quite beside the point, because our forefathers both thought and behaved in a manner that we can only term strategic, regardless of their cultural (including intellectual and linguistic) and contingent circumstances of time, place, and political identity.[54] Functionally, people acted politically with the tool of a strategic logic, long before the modern word for it was in widespread circulation. We can and should

46

approach strategic history with the eternal and ubiquitous functional logic of ends, ways, means—and assumptions, both as a critically important way of ensuring discipline in analyses, and for the promotion of understanding and usability for the products of our labor.

3. Science. There is much argument and ambiguity regarding the proper definition of science. Much of this ambiguity appears to be as inadvertent as it is unappreciated. Because definitions are discretionary and even somewhat arbitrary, it is particularly important to be clear as to what is meant by the noun science, or the adjective scientific, in a study such as this one. It is my contention that science requires the feasible pursuit of knowledge that can be considered to be true with a fair degree of certainty. This certainty can only be achieved when it is verifiable by empirical testing, or at least by direct reference to such. By definition, defense planning for future national security cannot be tested in a verifiable way. Our professional defense planners do their best to evade this temporal incapacity, given that such planning needs to be done, whether or not we know what we are doing. Soft social science strives for some understanding of the future that may be anticipated. However, this is not, by my definition, scientific understanding. Social science cannot produce predictions that can be verified to be true through testing. Because the descriptors, science and scientific, are held in high and wide respect in our society, there is nontrivial danger that social admiration for science will creep over whatever is claimed to be scientific. I suggest that much greater discipline should be exercised in consideration of what purports to be in some respect scientific, but which very often is nothing of the kind. There is no knowledge available to aid in guidance of defense and strategic planning for the future. Human choice, political circumstance, contingencies of many kinds in the future—none of these lend themselves to testable verification now. One may choose to be relaxed in one's understanding of science, and attempt to argue that science is only "disciplined thinking." Howard was not necessarily wrong when he said this back in 1973, but he did risk setting the bar unacceptably low.[55] After all, one can think with some discipline in a systematic manner, even if directly verifiable evidence is nowhere in sight. This monograph, therefore, recommends that the U.S. Army approaches future defense planning with a discipline unimpaired by ambiguity over what is and what is not known with certainty. It is especially important to appreciate that there is no magical method in science, let alone social science, that can possibly reveal the future reliably. The best we can do is employ our understanding of the past in a disciplined way.

4. Time. Military culture tends to be pragmatic, and heavily privileging, of discipline in the search for workable solutions, or work-arounds, to the problems of the day. Doctrine is both important and necessary for the routinization of those tasks that can be reduced to forms of a drill, provided imaginative answers to familiar, and especially unfamiliar, problems are not discouraged unduly as a result. The nurturing and honoring of tradition is important to military institutions for establishing and reinforcing pride in particular "tribal" identities. However, the pragmatic ethos that dominates institutions with jobs to do "now," can harmfully shorten the soldier's temporal horizon. This monograph has made many references to strategic history as comprising a continuous "stream of time" that should include past, present, and future. Because the future can provide no data to examine, we are reduced in our quest for evidence to the examination and exploitation of the past and (with serious reservations) the present.[56] It is ironic that a whole "stream of time" approach should be appropriate to the challenge of defense planning, even though this must owe nothing to knowledge of the future, which is always unavailable. My recommendation that the U.S. Army should be friendly to a view of strategic history sufficiently inclusive as to accommodate the future and founded on the conviction that problem-hopping is a systemic weakness in an institution culturally tilted strongly towards pragmatism. Because of the substantial changes in character of focus that the Army needs to make as real-world policy demands shift, there is a danger that "presentist" concerns and alarms may override somewhat competing requirements that seek to address the future, rather than the identified needs of today. This recommendation strives to be responsive to the whole problem area that is captured in the conceptual category of "change and continuity." The proposition key to the meaning of this fourth recommendation is that the proper temporal perspective for the U.S. Army is a great stream of time. The present and very near-term future must have high priority, but our history reveals in abundant empirical detail why national security tomorrow, in the future, always depends upon prudent preparation in the present day. This is not an exciting argument, but it has the unarguable merit of being true—and in this case, even scientifically testably so.

5. **Politics**. Strategy and its defense planning in the United States thoroughly depend upon the political process and the political skills of its operators. Members of the extended American defense community,

uniformed and civilian, can succumb to the error of believing that the requirements of military prudence are sufficiently comprehended by the electorate as to allow for a relaxed approach to strategic education. Furthermore, it tends to be forgotten by defense professionals that because strategy is really about politics, strategic education has to rest prudently on the education of those who are politically influential. This final recommendation truly is of fundamental importance, because it points with high confidence to the core of the subject. This is and has to be the relationship between the American political process and the motivations that shape and drive political will as policy, through and with strategy, to the zones of operational design and tactical action. Following Harold Lasswell, this monograph has argued that politics is about influence and the influential. How and why that matters most for the Army in the future is in respect to its then-contemporary meaning for the public American political "mood." That mood effectively will enable, disable or at least constrain, what a President wishes to do. Strategic and military experts in the United States should not be so blinded by their own understanding that they forget, or discount, the literally critical role played by the "mood" of electors as their representatives understand it. To be blunt, the U.S. Army will not be deployed or withheld from intervention abroad because the country will or will not need such a decision on objective and expertly considered grounds. Instead, the Army will be commanded to act only if and when the President is able to persuade, which is to say to influence, Congress that action is or is not required.[57] Regarded pragmatically and realistically, all decisions concerning the U.S. Army in the future — regarding preparation and action itself — has to be decided by our political process. That process is inherently innocent of foreign political, strategic, and military, content. An understanding of the future roles and relative high importance of the Army is not achieved by electors or their professional political representatives through some miraculous and mysterious process. Circumstances abroad to which we may well not have contributed, will likely explain why some apparent strategic dangers, and therefore challenges, evolve or erupt. But, the American public political "mood" usually needs expert domestic advice as fuel necessary for critical political decision.

ENDNOTES

1. I am grateful to Richard E. Neustadt and Ernest R. May for their exploration in *Thinking in Time: The Uses of History for Decision-Makers*, New York: Free Press, 1986, esp. Chap. 14. This book is of fundamental importance to my argument, and indeed to understanding the subject of defense planning.

2. Michael Howard, *The Lessons of History*, New Haven, CT: Yale University Press, 1999. Chap. 1, is outstandingly useful.

3. The eternal and ubiquitous adversarial nature of war, and therefore of preparation for its possibility, is suitably prominent on the first page of Carl von Clausewitz, *On War*, Michael Howard and Peter Paret, eds. and trans., Princeton, NJ: Princeton University Press, 1976, p. 75.

4. I explain the methodology problem fully in my *Strategy and Defence Planning: Meeting the Challenge of Uncertainty*, Oxford, United Kingdom (UK): Oxford University Press, forthcoming in 2014.

5. It is important for readers to understand that I require of science that it must be capable of achieving a certainty of understanding that can be tested, which is to say verified, empirically. Many people, and some professions and disciplines, choose to

be less rigorous in their requirements of "science" than am I. I am concerned that we do not dilute the standard demanded for knowledge to be described as "scientific."

6. It has been my first-hand experience both in London, UK, and Washington, DC, that sheer overfamiliarity with language can explain the casual undisciplined use of the word foreseeable. The very vagueness in the concept of a foreseeable future as it is used and misused, probably is key to explaining its persisting popularity. I did conceptual battle in Whitehall in the process that eventually produced Britain's latest *Strategic Defence and Security Review* in 2010, but I was not convinced, at the time or since, that my objection to the concept of a "foreseeable future" was fully understood by politicians and officials.

7. See Charles J. Hitch, *Decision-Making for Defense*, Berkeley, CA: University of California Press, 1965; Charles J. Hitch and Roland N. McKean, *The Economics of Defense in the Nuclear Age*, New York: Atheneum, 1966; Alain C. Enthoven and K. Wayne Smith, *How Much Is Enough? Shaping the Defense Program, 1961-1969*, Santa Monica, CA: RAND, 2005; and Alex Arbella, *Soldiers of Reason: The RAND Corporation and the Rise of the American Empire*, Orlando, FL: Harcourt, 2008.

8. For an excellent recent illustrative example of scenario design, see Andrew F. Krepinevich, *7 Deadly Scenarios: A Military Futurist Explores War in the 21st Century*, New York: Bantam Books, 2009.

9. Superior examples of trend analyses include United States Joint Forces Command (USJFCOM), *The Joint Operating Environment (JOE) 2010*, Suffolk, VA: U.S. Joint Forces Command, 2010; and U.K. Ministry of Defence, *Strategic Trends Programme: Global Strategic Trends – Out to 2040*, 4th Ed., London, UK: Development, Concepts, and Doctrine Centre (DCDC) for the Ministry of Defence, January 2010. USJFCOM has been disbanded, while it is unlikely that anyone responsible for the DCDC product of 2010 in the UK, will be overly troubled by a guilty conscience in 2040 for reason of inaccurate trend spotting.

10. Nassim Nicholas Taleb, *The Black Swan: The Impact of the Highly Improbable*, New York: Random House, 2010. A Black Swan

event is one that was not even considered possible, let alone likely, until it happened! Such mercifully very rare, but deeply consequential, surprises belong in or very close to the "unthinkable" range. Taleb's book is full of gems of logic that are relevant to all who attempt to understand the future—for which there is no direct evidence.

11. Probably the best illustration of the regularity of official error is provided in USJFCOM, "Strategic Estimates in the Twentieth Century," *The JOE 2010*, p. 9.

12. If one relaxes methodological discipline and admits that a theory can be both scientific yet tolerant of occasional eccentric misbehavior, the question of how much tolerance is permissible should not be ignored. The reason is not simply academic pedantry. A single event or episode in and of interstate war may occur in what supposed experts had believed was a period of deep peace. Even if it could be demonstrated empirically that large-scale interstate wars now belonged only in the past, that scientific truth, if such it is, could only pertain to the past and present of strategic history, not to the future. Taleb's *Black Swan* theory should be allowed to provide inspiration for prudent thought. The probability of occurrence of interstate nuclear war in the future is not calculable, whatever some scholars may believe. For an impressive and ruthless assault on the irrelevance of scientific method to prudent preparation for the future, see Jakub Grygiel, "Educating for National Security," *Orbis*, Vol. 57, No. 2, Spring 2013, pp. 201-206.

13. See Edward S. Quade, ed., *Analysis for Military Decisions: the RAND Lectures on Systems Analysis*, Chicago: RAND McNally, 1964; E. S. Quade and W. I. Boucher, eds., *Systems Analysis and Policy Planning: Applications in Defense*, New York: American Elsever Publishing Company, 1968; Enthoven and Smith, *How Much Is Enough?* and Glenn A. Kent, *Thinking About America's Defense: An Analytical Memoir*, Santa Monica, CA: RAND, 2008.

14. Unwarranted confidence in the ability of scientific analysis to bring truth to issues of national security continues to find devotees. See Michael O'Hanlon, *The Science of War: Defense Budgeting, Military Technology, Logistics, and Combat Outcomes*, Princeton, NJ: Princeton University Press, 2009, p. 1.

15. See Gregory A. Daddis, *No Sure Victory: Measuring U.S. Army Effectiveness and Progress in the Vietnam War*, Oxford, UK: Oxford University Press, 2011.

16. I have developed this metaphor in my book, *The Strategy Bridge: Theory for Practice*, Oxford, UK: Oxford University Press, 2010.

17. Grygiel, "Educating for National Security," is persuasive, to this strategist at least. Also see John Lewis Gaddis, *The Landscape of History: How Historians Map the Past,* Oxford, UK: Oxford University Press, 2002.

18. The reason why historical analogy cannot, or perhaps I ought to say should not, be employed to provide understanding by projection of inference about detail in the future, is explained with a robust clarity in David Hackett Fischer, *Historians' Fallacies: Toward a Logic of Historical Thought*, New York: Harper and Row, 1970, pp. 257-258, "The *fallacy of prediction by analogy*" (emphasis in the original).

19. Thucydides, *The Landmark Thucydides: A Comprehensive Guide to The Peloponnesian War,* Robert B. Strassler, ed., New York: Free Press, 1996, p.43; and Donald Rumsfeld, *Known and Unknown: A Memoir*, New York: Sentinel, 2011, pp. xiii-xiv.

20. Howard, *The Lessons of History*, p. 9.

21. Clausewitz, *On War*, pp. 88-89.

22. This claim for essential continuity in strategic history is developed in Colin S. Gray, *War, Peace and International Relations: An Introduction to Strategic History*, 2nd Ed., New York: Routledge, 2012.

23. Harold D. Lasswell, *Politics: Who Gets What, When, How*, Cleveland, OH: Meridian Books, 1958, p.13.

24. I pursue the large topics cited in this paragraph at considerable length in my forthcoming book, *Strategy and Defence Planning*.

25. Michael Howard, *The Causes of Wars*, London, UK: Counterpoint, 1983, p. 214.

> If there are no wars in the present in which the professional soldier can learn his trade, he is almost compelled to study the wars of the past. For after all allowances have been made for historical differences, wars still resemble each other more than they resemble any other human activity.

26. Vegetius, *Epitome of Military Science*, N. P. Milner, ed. and trans., Liverpool, UK: Liverpool University Press, 1993; Niccolo Machiavelli, *Art of War*, Christopher Lynch, ed. and trans., Chicago, IL: The University of Chicago Press, 2003. Also see Beatrice Heuser, *The Evolution of Strategy: Thinking War from Antiquity to the Present*, Cambridge, UK: Cambridge University Press, 2010, Chap. 3.

27. The outstanding study of this vital subject is Williamson Murray, *Military Adaptation in War: With Fear of Change*, Cambridge, UK: Cambridge University Press, 2011.

28. Clausewitz, *On War*, p. 104.

29. The classic statement of this eternal military and strategic truth was made, ironically, by a sailor! "*The ultimate determinant in war is the man on the scene with a gun*. This man is the final power in war. He is control. He determines who wins." (emphasis in the original). Rear Admiral J. C. Wylie, USN, *Military Strategy: A General Theory of Power Control*, Annapolis, MD: Naval Institute Press, 1989, p. 72.

30. See Robert Allan Doughty, *The Seeds of Disaster: The Development of French Army Doctrine, 1919-1939*, Hamdon, CT: Archon Books, 1985; Eugenia C. Kiesling, *Arming Against Hitler: France and the Limits of Military Planning*, Lawrence, KS: University Press of Kansas, 1996; and Elizabeth Keir, *Imagining War: French and British Military Doctrine Between the Wars*, Princeton, NJ: Princeton University Press, 1997.

31. In 1940 the French and the British were unfortunate in that they needed to cope with the finest military mind at the operational level that the whole of the war was to reveal: Erich von

Manstein. It was largely his operational concept that utterly un-hinged Anglo-French preparations and actions. Mungo Melvin, *Manstein: Hitler's Greatest General*, London, UK: Weidenfeld and Nicolson, 2010, is appropriately admiring both of German op-erational dexterity in May-June 1940, and of the quality of troop training achieved and subsequently demonstrated.

32. This proposition is thematic in the monumental military history by John France, *Perilous Glory: The Rise of Western Military Power*, New Haven, CT: Yale University Press, 2011, esp. Chap. 1.

33. The Strategic Air Command (SAC) was created, and re-designated, out of the Continental Air Forces of the US Army Air Force (USAAF). The early years of the SAC story and its challeng-es is well told in William S. Borgiasz, *The Strategic Air Command: Evolution and Consolidation of Nuclear Forces, 1945-1955*, Westport, CT: Praeger Publishers, 1996.

34. Howard, *The Causes of Wars*, p. 214.

35. "The whole of military activity must therefore relate di-rectly or indirectly to the engagement. The end of which a soldier is recruited, clothed, armed, and trained, the whole object of his sleeping, eating, drinking, and marching *is simply that he should fight at the right place and at the right time*" (emphasis in the origi-nal). Clausewitz, *On War*, p. 95.

36. I pursue this argument and relevant contextual consider-ations in my *Perspectives on Strategy*, Oxford, UK: Oxford Univer-sity Press, 2013, Chap. 5,

37. This point is made and developed in Colin S. Gray, *Mak-ing Strategic Sense of Cyber Power: Why the Sky Is Not Falling*, Car-lisle, PA: Strategic Studies Institute, U.S. Army War College, April 2013.

38. An unusual blend of mutually supporting granular mili-tary detail and strategic theory is provided in Emile Simpson's memoir-textbook on the conduct and misconduct of counterin-surgency warfare in Helmand Province, Afghanistan in the 2000s, *War from the Ground Up: Twenty-First Century Combat as Politics*, London, UK: Hurst, 2012.

39. See Athanassios G. Platias and Constantinos Koliopoulos, *Thucydides on Strategy: Athenian and Spartan Grand Strategies in the Peloponnesian War and their Relevance Today*, Athens, Greece: Eurasia Publications, 2006.

40. For detailed development of this argument, see Gray, *Strategy and Defence Planning*.

41. See Endnote 29.

42. There is high value in Ken Booth, *Strategy and Ethnocentrism*, London, UK: Croom Helm, 1979. A 2nd Edition of this deeply insightful book is forthcoming soon from Routledge.

43. By way of illustration, see Nigel Bagnall, *The Punic Wars: Rome, Carthage, and the Struggle for the Mediterranean*, London, UK: Pimlico, 1999; Clifford J. Rogers, *War Cruel and Sharp: English Strategy under Edward III, 1327-1360*, Woodbridge, UK: The Boydell Press, 2000; Richard Holmes, *Marlborough: England's Fragile Genius*, London, UK: Harper Press, 2008; and Huw J. Davies, *Wellington's Wars: The Making of a Military Genius*, New Haven, CT: Yale University Press, 2012.

44. See Donald W. Engels, *Alexander the Great and the Logistics of the Macedonian Army*, Berkeley, CA: University of California Press, 1978. To advance historical grasp closer to today, also see Martin van Creveld, *Supplying War: Logistics from Wallenstein to Patton,* Cambridge, UK: Cambridge University Press, 1977; and Thomas M. Kane, *Military Logistics and Strategic Performance*, London, UK: Frank Cass, 2001.

45. Frederick F. Cartwright and Michael Biddiss, *Disease and History,* Stroud, UK: Sutton Publishing, 2000, scans much of this subject of concern, while John M. Barry, *The Great Influenza: The Epic Story of the Deadliest Plague in History,* London, UK: Penguin Books, 2005, did not really require the exciting, but almost certainly accurate, claim in its secondary title.

46. Clausewitz, *On War*, pp.119-121.

47. See Lasswell, *Politics*. For the full story told in historical perspective, see Alan Ryan, *On Politics: A History of Po-*

litical Thought from Herodotus to the Present, London, UK: Allan Lane, 2012.

48. Williamson Murray, *War, Strategy, and Military Effectiveness,* Cambridge, UK: Cambridge University Press, 2011, p. 33.

49. See Taleb, *The Black Swan.*

50. Henry D. Sokolski and Bruno Tetrais, eds., *Nuclear Weapons Security Crises: What Does History Teach?* Carlisle, PA: Strategic Studies Institute and U.S. Army War College Press, July 2013. For a broader view, see Jeremy Black, *Using History*, London, UK: Hodder Arnold, 2005, is a wide ranging and useful discussion.

51. This opinion derived from my experience both as a participant and subsequently as a scholar. See my book, *House of Cards: Why Arms Control Must Fail*, Ithaca, NY: Cornell University Press, 1992.

52. All that was wrong with the theory of arms control was the empirically well-attested fact that it does not work well in practice. The most impressive works that founded the modern theory of arms control were Hedley Bull, *The Control of the Arms Race: Disarmament and Arms Control in the Missile Age,* London, UK: Weidenfeld and Nicolson for the Institute for Strategic Studies, 1961; and Thomas C. Schelling and Morton H. Halperin, *Strategy and Arms Control*, New York: Twentieth Century Fund, 1961.

53. A powerful and compelling recent example of COIN scepticism is Gian Gentile, *Wrong Turn: America's Deadly Embrace of Counterinsurgency*, New York: The New Press, 2013. Colonel Gentile's case is sufficiently strong that eschewal of high voltage wording in its book's title would probably have been advisable.

54. See Heuser, *The Evolution of Strategy*, Chap. 1; and Gray, *The Strategy Bridge: Theory for Practice*, Appendix C, "Conceptual 'Hueys' at Thermopylae? The Challenge of Strategic Anachronism," pp. 266-277.

55. Michael Howard, "Military Science in an Age of Peace," *The RUSI Journal*, Vol. 119, No. 1, March 1974, p. 4.

56. The most obvious limitation to the value of present day experience is the total unavailability of any audit of effectiveness based on verifiable, or even plausible, consequences.

57. The legal fact that the President is Commander-in-Chief has been eroded recently in its interpretation as the license to initiate military action on the basis of his constitutional discretion.

U.S. ARMY WAR COLLEGE

Major General Anthony A. Cucolo III
Commandant

*****

STRATEGIC STUDIES INSTITUTE
and
U.S. ARMY WAR COLLEGE PRESS

Director
Professor Douglas C. Lovelace, Jr.

Director of Research
Dr. Steven K. Metz

Author
Dr. Colin S. Gray

Editor for Production
Dr. James G. Pierce

Publications Assistant
Ms. Rita A. Rummel

*****

Composition
Mrs. Jennifer E. Nevil

www.ingramcontent.com/pod-product-compliance
Lightning Source LLC
Chambersburg PA
CBHW081722270326

41933CB00017B/3260